D0412768

THE
ARAB-ISRAELI
CONFLICT

IVAN MINNIS

Heinemann
LIBRARY

www.heinemann.co.uk
Visit our website to find out more information about **Heinemann Library** books.

To order:
 Phone 44 (0) 1865 888066
 Send a fax to 44 (0) 1865 314091
Visit the Heinemann Bookshop at www.heinemann.co.uk to browse our catalogue and order online.

First published in Great Britain by Heinemann Library, Halley Court, Jordan Hill, Oxford OX2 8EJ, a division of Reed Educational and Professional Publishing Ltd.
Heinemann is a registered trademark of Reed Educational and Professional Publishing Ltd.

OXFORD MELBOURNE AUCKLAND JOHANNESBURG BLANTYRE GABORONE
IBADAN PORTSMOUTH (NH) USA CHICAGO

Designed by AMR
Illustrated by Chartwell Illustrators
Originated by Dot Gradations
Printed by South China Printers

05 04 03 02
10 9 8 7 6 5 4 3 2
ISBN 0 431 11861 2 (hardback)

05 04 03 02
10 9 8 7 6 5 4 3 2 1
ISBN 0 431 11867 1 (paperback)

British Library Cataloguing in Publication Data

Minnis, Ivan
  The Arab-Israeli conflict. – (Troubled world)
  1.Arab-Israeli conflict – Juvenile literature
  I.Title
  956'.04

Acknowledgements
The publishers would like to thank the following for permission to reproduce photographs:
Pg.5 Rex Features/S Frischling; Pg.7 Rex Features; Pg.9 Popperfoto; Pg.11 [top] Spaarnestad Fotoarchief [bottom] Hulton Getty/Hans Haim Pinn Photoservice; Pg.13 Popperfoto; Pg.15 Rex Features; Pg.17 Hulton Getty; Pg.18 Popperfoto; Pg.19 Popperfoto; Pg.20 Popperfoto; Pg.22 Associated Press; Pg.25 Hulton Getty; Pg.26 Hulton Getty; Pg.28 Hulton Getty; Pg.30 Hulton Getty; Pg.31 Popperfoto; Pg.33 Hulton Getty; Pg.35 Rex Features/Sipa Press; Pg.36 Popperfoto; Pg.37 Rex Features; Pg.38 Popperfoto; Pg.41 Hulton Getty; Pg.42 Popperfoto/Reuters; Pg.44 Rex Features/Sipa Press; Pg.46 Rex Features; Pg.47 Los Angeles Times; Pg.48 Popperfoto; Pg.51 Rex Features/Villard; Pg.52 Rex Features/Reardon; Pg.54 Popperfoto; Pg.55 Popperfoto; Pg.57 Press Association; Pg.58 European Press Agency.

Cover photograph reproduced with permission of Panos Pictures.

Every effort has been made to contact copyright holders of any material reproduced in this book. Any omissions will be rectified in subsequent printings if notice is given to the publishers.

Contents

Words that appear in the text in bold, **like this**, are explained in the glossary.

The Struggle in the Middle East

The Middle East is an area extending from the Persian Gulf to the eastern end of the Mediterranean. For centuries **nomadic** tribes roamed its deserts and plains in search of grazing for their livestock, occasionally settling around an oasis or river to build the ancient towns and cities that still stand today. Three continents, Europe, Asia and Africa, meet in the Middle East, which helped the region to become a centre for trade and learning in ancient times. Its rivers and seas formed trade routes bringing exotic spices and incense from the Far East and Africa to Western Europe and beyond. Trading encouraged the spread of new ideas and the area became the home of three of the world's major religions: Christianity, **Islam** and **Judaism**. The importance each faith places on the area has led to conflict for centuries.

During the 19th century the construction of the Suez Canal, connecting the Mediterranean and Red Seas, increased the region's importance as a trade route, with the canal providing new and faster routes from Europe to India and the Pacific. However, the discovery of vast quantities of oil in the area during the 20th century made the Middle East more significant than ever. Without oil from the region, the **developed world** would grind to a halt. World leaders therefore watch closely each new development in the region.

The emergence of Israel

The 20th century saw the break-up of the once great **Ottoman Empire**, with many **Arab** nations gaining their independence. At the same time the new state of Israel was created with many **Jews** returning to their ancient homeland. Their arrival in the region angered many Arabs, who regarded their Jewish neighbours as a threat to Arab unity. The creation of Israel in 1948 brought war, with Arab nations determined to crush the new state before it could take root. Israel was able to survive but thousands of **Palestinians** were forced to live in refugee camps in neighbouring states. Over the next fifty years war and violence became common, with the existence of the state of Israel a constant point of conflict in the region. Inevitably the international community has found itself being drawn into this conflict, often with terrible consequences.

American Jews protest against the peace negotiations between Shimon Peres and Yasser Arafat.

Superpower rivalry

Israel emerged as an independent state at the end of the 1940s, a time when the Second World War alliance of the United States and the Soviet Union was beginning to disintegrate. The tense relationship between these two great **superpowers** led to the **Cold War**. Both sides wanted to increase their power but the threat of nuclear weapons made it impossible for direct conflict between them. Instead they tried to extend their influence over other nations by providing them with weapons and financial aid. In doing so they hoped to befriend governments so that they would support them in times of crisis.

The new countries of the Middle East soon found themselves at the centre of this superpower rivalry. The United States has been very supportive of Israel, with America's large Jewish population lobbying for support of the new state. The US also tried to maintain friendly governments in some Arab states, such as Saudi Arabia. Meanwhile the Soviet Union extended its influence amongst other Arab countries, such as Syria and Egypt, providing them with weapons and aid in their attempt to defeat Israel.

Trade

The construction of the Suez Canal during the mid 19th century opened up the Red Sea and Indian Ocean to European ships sailing out of the Mediterranean. The canal was of particular importance to the British who regarded it as a vital route to parts of their Empire such as India and Australia. A desire to keep control of this canal, and to maintain a friendly government in Egypt, was central to Britain's involvement in the early years of the **Arab**-Israeli struggle.

Oil

The discovery of vast quantities of oil in the region increased the importance of the Middle East. Arab states, aware of the power their oil gives them, have limited production during times of crisis, forcing western powers to intervene and put pressure on Israel. Arab use of this 'oil weapon' (for instance see pages 30–31) has ensured that developed nations cannot afford to ignore instability and conflict in the area.

American involvement in the Middle East

As you will see later in the book, the United States, Soviet Union and **United Nations (UN)** have intervened in several of the wars and crises that have developed between the Arab states and the Israelis. Many Arab states have resented this interference, especially that of the United States. As a result some are willing to give support to **Islamic** groups that use terrorism and hostage taking to highlight their stand against Israel. For many of these groups, US support for Israel makes American **citizens**, both military and **civilian**, targets for terrorist attack.

The US has shown itself willing to intervene against terrorism. In 2001, President Bush launched a 'war on terrorism' following devastating attacks on American cities by Islamic terrorists.

'A fifth day of fierce clashes between Israelis and Palestinians left at least 13 more people dead – the death toll from five days of violence has reached at least 50.'
A report by BBC World Service on 3 October 2000. Such reports have been all too common in more than 50 years of conflict.

The international community

The Arab-Israeli conflict has raged for over fifty years despite the intervention of many western governments and the UN. UN peacekeepers have been based on the Sinai Peninsula and in Beirut in an attempt to prevent the conflict escalating. Meanwhile it has been at the centre of diplomatic moves to try to find a resolution to the conflict. The United States has also pushed hard for a solution, often pressing their Israeli allies into negotiations.

Jerusalem: the Holy City

During the reign of King Solomon, around 1000BC, a great building programme was undertaken in Jerusalem. The most significant building erected was the Great Temple, the centre of **Judaism**. The temple was destroyed by the Romans during the first **Jewish** revolt of AD70 and eventually built over, leaving only the 'Wailing Wall', the holiest site for modern Jews.

The city also has great significance for **Muslims**. They believe that at the end of the prophet Mohammed's life he was miraculously taken from Mecca to Jerusalem. From there he ascended in seven stages into heaven. Both sides therefore regard Jerusalem as central to their faith and control of the city is of great importance.

The Old City of Jerusalem. The Mosque of the Dome, one of Islam's most holy sites, can be seen rising above the Walled City.

7

The Holy Land 1: The Jews

The state of Israel is one of the world's newest countries but the land has a long and troubled history. Both **Jews** and **Arabs** claim to be the rightful owners of the land and each states that their religion and history justify their presence.

The Jews

The Old Testament tells the story of how Abraham made an agreement with God, which promised him and his descendants the ancient land of Canaan. The 'promised land' was colonized by Abraham's descendants, his son Jacob, who was also known as Israel, providing the name for the new 'Israelites'.

The Bible also tells how the Israelites were forced by famine to leave their land in around 2000BC and settle in Egypt. The Pharaohs enslaved them until Moses led them home in around 1300BC. A further time of **exile** followed in the 6th century BC, this time in Babylonia (roughly modern Iraq and Syria), but again the Israelites were able to return to their homeland, now known as Palestine.

During the 1st century BC Palestine was invaded by the Romans. The Jews could not accept the many Roman Gods or the culture of the Empire. Their rebellions were put down with great violence that saw the destruction of Jerusalem and its Great Temple. Again the Jews were exiled and scattered across Europe where they would be less troublesome to their rulers. They would not return for almost 2000 years.

The Jews in exile

Following their exile by the Romans, the Jews were unable to find a welcoming home anywhere in Europe. Christians regarded them with suspicion and hatred. These were the people, they said, who had called for Christ's crucifixion. The Jews maintained their customs and religion, making them different from their neighbours and therefore strange people who provided easy scapegoats in times of crisis. Jews were blamed for the plague, the disappearance of children and political plots. Thus, from time to time throughout the following centuries, they met with persecution. They were expelled from England in 1292 and from Spain in 1492 and met with great persecution during the 1880s in Russia. A series of bloody attacks across Russia, known as **'pogroms'**, left thousands dead.

Theodor Herzl, the father of modern Zionism.

Zionism

The Russian pogroms left many Jews believing that they could only live in peace if they were able to return to their homeland. This belief became known as **Zionism**, from the old Jewish name for Palestine, Zion.

Jews began to drift back to Palestine in 1882, setting up a colony near the city of Jaffa. Money from rich supporters enabled more to follow. Their leader was Theodor Herzl, a Hungarian Jew who wanted a separate Jewish state to allow his people to escape **anti-semitism** in Europe. This state, he suggested, could be in Palestine or Argentina. At the first Zionist Congress, in 1897, it was agreed that Palestine was the better option and a fund was set up to buy land for Jewish settlers.

The events of the Second World War proved still further the need for a homeland. The persecution of centuries reached its climax with the **Holocaust**. The Nazis, feeding off the widespread European anti-semitism, murdered over six million Jews in extermination camps such as Auschwitz. Those Jews who remained had lost everything: homes, families, businesses and, perhaps most importantly, their trust in their European neighbours. They were more determined than ever to start new lives in Palestine.

The **Holocaust** also stirred the leaders of the west into action. As evidence of the Holocaust filtered into the media, public sympathy came in firmly behind the **Jews**. This was especially true in the USA, which had a large and powerful Jewish community. Jewish immigration to Palestine rocketed and Britain was powerless to prevent the country sliding into a conflict that has continued for almost 50 years.

A siege society

Early Jewish victories were no guarantee of the survival of their young country. Israel is surrounded by its **Arab** neighbours, military powers who are openly hostile to the Israelis. As a result Israel is a nation which regards itself as being under constant threat of attack. The memories of the Holocaust are fresh and Israel is determined to take measures to defend itself, regardless of the opinions of either the Middle East or the rest of the world. They have therefore been prepared to seize land in other countries – Egypt, Jordan and Lebanon – in order to create **'buffer zones'** that lessen the impact of any Arab attack. Jerusalem has become a symbol of independence and determination to survive in the face of widespread opposition and hostility.

An Orthodox or a secular society

The early Zionists believed 'Jewish' described a national identity. In 1948, the then Prime Minister David Ben-Gurion signed the 'religious status quo' agreement. It required that the Sabbath (Saturday) and Kashrut (Jewish dietary law) be officially observed in the state. Civil marriages were not allowed and the Ultra-**Orthodox** were provided with an independent educational system. This was designed to appease the Orthodox Jews who maintain strict observance of religious laws.

However, since then, Israel's population has grown and changed. While Orthodox Jews make up 20 to 30 per cent of the population, **secular** Jews and ethnically Russian and Ethiopian Jews find the laws a burden on their daily life. This divide has important implications for the peace process. Orthodox Jews and their sympathizers in the **Knesset** (the Israeli Parliament) are strongly opposed to negotiations with the **Palestinians** and form a powerful lobby in the country.

Prisoners being liberated from Dachau concentration camp at the end of the Second World War

'Next year in Jerusalem'

A return to their ancient homeland in Palestine has always been at the heart of the Jewish faith. For centuries Jews throughout the world consoled themselves at **Passover** festivals with the prayer, 'Next year in Jerusalem'. The terrible events of the Holocaust made the Jews even more determined to have their own state, and to defend it once achieved. One Israeli broadcaster summed up this strength of feeling: 'I don't believe in the Jews' historical right to take land from other people because we were here 2000 years ago. We have the right because of the Holocaust.'

The ship, *Jewish State* arriving in Haifa with 2000 Jewish refugees on board. World sympathy for the Jews was aroused when the British, who feared Arab violence, turned it away.

The Holy Land 2: The Arabs

The 7th century AD saw the development of a new religion in the Middle East: **Islam**. The prophet Mohammed, born in Mecca in AD570, brought this new religion to the **Arab** people. To the Arabs, Mohammed was the greatest of all prophets and after his death their armies began to spread his ideas throughout the Middle East and North Africa. For 500 years the Arabs ruled a great empire, extending from Spain to India and taking in Palestine but, after centuries of decline, they eventually came under Turkish rule in the 16th century. Unlike the **Jews**, however, the Arabs remained in Palestine.

Arab nationalism

By 1914 the Arab people had been ruled by the Turks for 400 years. They felt that their culture and economic development had been held back by the Turks, leaving them poor and backward. So, when Turkey sided with Germany in the First World War, the Arabs were only too willing to join with Britain in an attempt to free their country.

In return for Arab support, Britain promised to help set up an Arab state in the Middle East, which the Arabs assumed would include Palestine. The inter-war period did not bring Arab independence, however. Instead, the **League of Nations** put the region in the hands of European powers. British control of Palestine saw the start of large-scale Jewish immigration into the country, with an often violent response from the Arab community. After one particularly horrific attack on Jewish settlers in 1929, the British enquiry concluded that 'the **Palestinians** have come to see [the Jews] not only as a menace to their livelihood but a possible overlord of the future'. The report turned out to be prophetic.

A people without a homeland

In 1948, there were approximately 860,000 Palestinians inside today's Israel. About 700,000 were driven out or fled during the fighting that followed the declaration of Israeli statehood. The Palestinian population of Jerusalem went from 75,000 to 3500; of Jaffa from 70,000 to 3600; of Haifa from 71,000 to 2900. The refugees were dispersed into camps in neighbouring Arab states. The 160,000 Palestinians still in Israel in 1949 lost much of their land leaving them with no resources or strong leaders.

Refugees at Ramallah in 1948. Thousands of Palestinians fled their homes, their families forced to remain in camps for the next 50 years.

Although defeated in the 1948 war, the Palestinians have refused to accept the new state of Israel. Like the Jews of the **Diaspora** they now dream of a return to their homeland. In his address to the **United Nations** in 1974 Yasser Arafat made clear the Palestinian position: 'It [the conflict] is the cause of a people deprived of its homeland, dispersed and uprooted, living mostly in **exile** and in refugee camps'. The anthem of the **Palestinian Liberation Organization (PLO)** goes further: 'Palestine is our country. Our aim is to return. Death does not frighten us, Palestine is ours'.

Other Arab groupings

Aside from the PLO, other Palestinian and **Islamic guerrilla** groups have influenced the conflict:

- The Popular Front for the Liberation of Palestine and the Black September Organization both emerged in the early 1970s, carrying out infamous terrorist attacks such as the kidnapping of Israeli athletes at the Munich Olympics in 1972.
- The 1982 Israeli invasion of the Lebanon saw the appearance of Islamic **militia** groups such as Hezbollah and Amal who have targeted Israel and the United States.
- During the 1987 **Intifada**, a new Palestinian group, Hamas, was formed by Palestinians unhappy with the more moderate approach adopted by the PLO. It has substantial support in the **Occupied Territories**, and is viewed as a threat to the peace process.

The Palestinian Liberation Organization

In 1964 the **Arab** states created the **Palestine Liberation Organization (PLO)**. While it was supposed to represent the **Palestinians**, it really represented the views of President Nasser of Egypt. Its first leader made wild threats to drive the Israelis into the sea, but he had little support among Palestinians for he was seen as a puppet of the Egyptians. His threat was never taken seriously by Israeli leaders but provided them with useful propaganda, especially in the US. In the 1960s Palestinian students began to form their own organizations independent of control by Arab governments (although the Syrians, Libyans, and Iraqis continued to fund and control particular groups). Yasser Arafat, who ran an engineering firm in Kuwait, founded an independent Palestinian-run party called Fatah. In the late 1960s Arafat emerged as the principal leader of the Palestinian people.

Under Arafat's leadership the PLO has adopted a variety of tactics throughout the conflict. Regarded by some as freedom fighters and by others as terrorists, it has fought pitched battles with the Israelis, as well as using bombing campaigns, hijacking and assassination to further its cause.

Since the late 1980s the organization has moved towards more moderate policies. Rather than wanting to destroy Israel, it has entered into talks aimed at achieving a negotiated settlement. It is now effectively regarded by all in the talks as the voice of the Palestinian people and assumed control of parts of the **Occupied Territories** after the Oslo Peace Accords in 1993.

Profile: Yasser Arafat (1929–)

While studying for an engineering degree in Cairo during the 1960s Yasser Arafat helped found Fatah, a Palestinian guerrilla group. Soon after, Fatah became part of the PLO, effectively its military wing, and Arafat was made overall leader of the PLO in 1969. In 1974 he addressed the **UN** General Assembly, famously with a pistol strapped to his waist. He promised further violence unless a Palestinian state was created.

The campaign did continue, but Arafat's position as leader was far from secure when the 1982 Israeli invasion of the Lebanon forced him from his Beirut base. However, he remained in control and, from 1988 onwards, led the PLO towards negotiations with Israel. Arafat fell out of favour with the international community for his support of Iraq during the Gulf War, but the successful negotiations that led to the Oslo Peace Accords restored his credibility. In 1994, a year after formally signing up to the Accords in Washington, Arafat was awarded the Nobel Peace Prize along with the Israeli Prime Minister Yitzhak Rabin and his Foreign Minister Shimon Peres.

Although Arafat became President of the Palestinian Authority in 1996, continued attacks on Israel by extreme Palestinian groups have put his position under pressure.

Yasser Arafat, President of the Palestinian Authority.

Turning Point: The British Mandate and the Creation of Israel

The Balfour Declaration

In November 1917 the British Foreign Secretary, Arthur Balfour, wrote to leading **Zionists** declaring that Britain would support their plans for a homeland in Palestine. **Arabs** were furious, knowing that if this was the case it would be at the expense of their people in Palestine. Britain assured them that plans for a united Arab state were unaffected, but nevertheless continued to favour the Zionist demands.

The Treaty of Versailles

Britain's attitude became of greater importance after the First World War. The Treaty of Versailles gave control of much of Turkey's Middle Eastern empire to the British. The peacemakers wanted the peoples of the defeated empire to be able to rule themselves, but felt that they were not yet ready. Britain ruled the area as a 'mandate', preparing the people for self-government. To **Jews** the **British Mandate** appeared to be an opportunity to put their plans into action.

The British Mandate

The years of British Rule in Palestine saw increasing violence, as Arabs reacted angrily to the arrival of Jewish settlers, with immigration figures set at 16,500. Arab riots in 1921 led to a reduction in the number of Jews allowed into Palestine but the number of Zionist settlements continued to grow. In 1929 extreme Zionists demonstrating near the Mosque of the Dome in Jerusalem also led to mass rioting by Arabs in which over a hundred Jews were killed.

With Hitler's rise to power in Germany, even more Jews fled Europe and immigration rose to 61,000 in 1935. The Arab leaders called a General Strike in an attempt to force a change in British policy. They were successful, but the change was not what they desired. The British announced that Palestine would be divided into an Arab and a Jewish state, with half of the country allocated to the Zionists. The Arabs immediately rebelled but, by 1939, had been defeated by stronger British forces. The outbreak of the Second World War in September 1939 temporarily united most Jews and Arabs behind the British, but the problem had not been resolved. The terrible events of the **Holocaust** were about to transform both Europe and the Middle East.

The Arabs continued to resist British rule even after their decisive defeat in 1939.

On 22 July 1946 a bomb exploded in the King David Hotel, headquarters of the British military in Palestine. Members of 'Irgun', a Jewish terrorist group, disguised as Arabs, had driven it up to the hotel's kitchen. The resulting explosion killed 88 people, including 15 Jews. The bomb clearly demonstrated the lengths to which Zionists would go to expel the British from Palestine in their desire to create a homeland for the Jews.

The violence continued as the British attempted to limit the number of Jews gaining entry to Palestine, people turning their backs on Europe after the horrors of the Holocaust. Eventually, in February 1947, the British announced plans to withdraw, unable to sustain troop levels of 100,000 in the **austere** post-war years. Instead it was proposed that Palestine would be handed over to the control of the **United Nations**.

Partition

The UN decided that the only possible solution was to divide Palestine into separate Jewish and Arab states. Although they made up only one third of the population, the Jews were to be given a greater share of the land in anticipation of more immigration. Inevitably the Arabs rejected the plan, not wanting to give up so much of their land. The Jews and the Holocaust, it was argued were the responsibility of Europe, not of the Arabs. Palestinian Jews were also unhappy with the proposed boundaries as they left Jerusalem in the heart of the Arab zone. The holy city of three religions would come under the control of the UN but control of the access roads was in Arab hands.

A member of the Haganah on sentry duty during the 1948 war.

War of liberation

In the build up to British withdrawal violence between the **Jews** and **Arabs** increased as both sides tried to gain control of the roads leading to Jerusalem. Soldiers from Syria and Iraq prepared to come to the aid of their Arab neighbours while the Jewish **Haganah** organized the defence of Jewish areas. More extreme elements within the Jewish community began to attack Arab settlements. By the time the British withdrew in May 1948, more than 300,000 Arabs had fled Jewish areas.

War of Liberation

'Tens of thousands of our youth are prepared to lay down their lives for the sake of Jerusalem. It is within the boundaries of the state of Israel just as Tel Aviv is.'
David Ben-Gurion, first Prime Minister of Israel

Year of Catastrophe

'The Palestinian problem is the story of a people who lived peacefully in their own homes for generations. Then along came total strangers who turned the people out of their country and occupied their homes.'
S Hadawi, an Arab Writer

Despite initial confidence and optimism, the Arab forces were disorganized and had difficulty defending the long borders of the Arab zone. The Haganah, operating from the much smaller area which they controlled, was able to first resist the Arab onslaught and then drive them back, capturing large parts of what the **UN** had declared to be Arab territory. By January of 1949 the two sides came to an uneasy truce and the state of Israel had survived its first assault.

Year of Catastrophe

While to the Jews 1948 was a year of liberation, to the Arabs it became their 'Year of Catastrophe'. Thousands died in the fighting, some in horrific massacres. In April 1948 around 80 members of the Irgun, led by the future Prime Minister of Israel, Menachim Begin, attacked the Arab village of Deir Yassin. They killed the entire population of the village, leading to widespread panic among the Arab population. Around 700,000 Arabs fled their homes as further areas of Palestine came under Jewish control. Defeated in the civil war, the **Palestinians** were now a people without a homeland. They were forced to seek sanctuary in neighbouring Arab states. These former allies found it difficult to absorb these refugees, who were not assimilated into the local population. Instead the Palestinians lived in huge refugee camps close to the Israeli border, waiting for an opportunity to regain their lands.

Profile: David Ben-Gurion 1886–1973

Ben-Gurion was born in Poland but emigrated to Palestine in 1906. He helped organize the Haganah, the secret Jewish defence force of the 1930s and 40s. He came to prominence as a **Zionist** spokesman between 1942 and 1948, proclaiming Israel a new state on British withdrawal. He was Prime Minister from 1948 to 1953, and from 1955 to 1963 and is regarded as the architect of modern Israel.

David Ben-Gurion, proclaiming the birth of the new Jewish state, 24 May 1948.

The Suez-Sinai War of 1956

After its victory in the war of independence the new state of Israel was weak and surrounded by enemies. The homeland dreamt of by the **Zionists** opened its doors to **Jews** from all over Europe and the Middle East. By the end of 1951 657,000 Jews had swelled the population, immigrants as committed to **Zionism** as their predecessors. Slowly, supported by the wealth of the USA, the fledgling state was able to grow in confidence.

The Arab reaction

The **Arab** world had been stunned by its defeat in the war of independence. Old regimes were replaced with more **nationalistic** young leaders who wanted to modernize their countries. These leaders turned against the West, particularly the USA and Britain, regarding them as interfering Zionists. They aimed instead to create a united Arab world able to act together in areas of common interest.

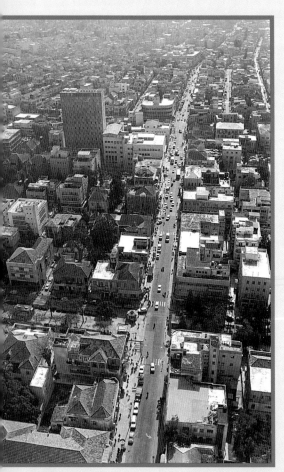

The **Palestinians**, meanwhile, found themselves a people without a state. Their Arab neighbours refused to grant them **citizenship**, condemning them to a future in refugee camps. Some were prepared to fight to regain their lands. The **Fedayeen** (Arabic for 'self-sacrificers') launched attacks against the Israelis almost as soon as the war of independence ended. The Israelis hit back, attacking not only the Fedayeen but also their Arab neighbours. With each passing year the Fedayeen attacks and Israeli **reprisals** further heightened tensions in the Middle East.

Tel Aviv, home of the Knesset, the Israeli parliament.

Nasser and Arab nationalism

In Egypt in 1952 young army officers overthrew the corrupt pro-British regime of King Farouk. Two years later Colonel Nasser took control, forcing a British withdrawal from their positions around the Suez Canal, a vital trade route for oil from the region. Nasser immediately began an extensive programme of modernization. Factories, hospitals and schools were built, with plans for a huge dam at Aswan put in place to provide more agricultural land.

Relationships between Egypt and the western powers became increasingly strained under Nasser. In 1955, under pressure from those in his government who wanted a stronger military, he turned to the Soviet Union for arms supplies. Britain and the USA feared that the Soviet Union was attempting to gain influence in the Middle East. They showed their anger by cancelling loans offered to support Nasser's most prestigious project, the Aswan Dam.

The Suez Canal

The Suez Canal is an important trade route, linking the Mediterranean Sea to the Indian Ocean. Without it, ships sailing from Europe to the Far East would be forced to sail around the south of Africa, adding thousands of miles to their journeys. Until 1956 Britain and France owned the canal.

When the loans for the Aswan dam were cancelled, Nasser reacted swiftly, announcing that he would nationalize the canal. Instead of its profits going to Britain and France, Egypt would use the money to help pay for the country's modernization. This was the last straw for the British and French. They regarded the canal as vital to their navies and trade, and feared that Nasser might close it to them, or use it as a bargaining tool. The two governments decided that Nasser had to be overthrown but could not risk angering other Arab states.

Knowing that they could not invade Egypt themselves the British and French governments entered into secret negotiations with Israel. A plan emerged for Israel to attack Egypt, destroying the Fedayeen in Sinai and advancing to the Suez Canal. Britain and France would then demand that both sides had to withdraw from the canal zone. If, as they expected, Nasser refused to withdraw they would send in troops, claiming that they were there to stop the fighting and keep the canal open. The plan had risks. Britain and France insisted on keeping the plan a secret from the Americans, who had warned them not to use force in the region. The Israelis feared that its secrecy would anger the Americans, who had supported them since 1945. However, their Prime Minister, David Ben-Gurion, thought it important to strike against Egypt and was willing to accept French weapons which would allow him to do so.

The fighting begins

On 29 October 1956 Israel sent its troops into the Sinai Peninsula. Egyptian communications had been cut and Israeli forces were able to make great gains in the area. As planned, Britain and France demanded that both sides should withdraw 16 kilometres

Colonel Gamal Abdel Nasser.

from the Suez Canal. When Nasser refused, air-strikes were launched against Egypt's airfields, destroying many planes on the ground. Free from air attacks, the Israeli forces were able to occupy most of Sinai before British and French paratroopers landed to the North at Port Said.

Profile: Colonel Gamal Abdel Nasser (1918–1970)

The son of a post office clerk, Nasser became an officer in the Egyptian Army in 1938. He was angered by Egypt's failure to defeat Israel in 1948 and masterminded the 1952 plot which overthrew King Farouk. As President he introduced reforms that improved life for ordinary Egyptians but he was unable to create the United **Arab** Republic he hoped for, with his military dependence on the Soviet Union worrying many Arab leaders. Egypt's crushing defeat by Israel in 1967 reduced his influence in the Arab world, but he remained popular at home until his death in 1970.

The aftermath

Although the military campaign appeared to be going well for Britain, France and Israel, there was an international outcry over their actions. In Britain, public opinion was against the attack and the government itself came under attack from all sides. The United States government was furious and, through the **United Nations** Security Council, demanded an immediate **ceasefire**. The British and French **vetoed** the proposal.

With the western powers in disarray, the Soviet Union made it clear that it was prepared to send troops into the area to assist Egypt. America could not risk such a move so threatened to withdraw oil supplies to Britain and France. With supplies from Arab states drying up, the two governments were forced into an embarrassing withdrawal with United Nations peacekeepers taking over their positions along the canal.

Results of the war

The Suez-Sinai war was a complete disaster for Britain and France. Britain's decline as a world power was clear as was its reliance on the United States. Britain's role and influence in the Middle East were greatly reduced as Arab states turned instead to the Soviet Union for backing. Pro-British Arab States, such as Iraq and the Lebanon, turned against them, leaving America to try to keep a check on Soviet influence.

For Israel the war was a military success. They had defeated the Egyptians and crushed the **Fedayeen**. In January 1957 they were forced by the UN to withdraw from the Sinai Peninsula but, despite losing their territorial gains, they had still improved their position. A UN peacekeeping force patrolled the Sinai border, preventing further Arab attacks in the area and reopening the Gulf of Aqaba to Israeli shipping.

Although defeated in the war, Nasser's reputation as leader of the Arab world grew. He was respected for standing up to the western powers and winning a diplomatic victory. With Nasser at its head, it appeared possible that the Arab world would soon fall under the influence of the Soviet Union.

The Six-Day War

Between 1956 and 1967 an uneasy peace prevailed in the Middle East. In Israel there were signs that the country was struggling to cope with its independence. The economy was in difficulty and unemployment high. There were many strikes and demands for higher wages. Politically, things were also very uncertain. It was time for the new, younger men to take over but there was no obvious successor to Ben-Gurion and this caused a terrible feeling of insecurity. So, while to the outside world, things seemed to be well – unified and progressive – all was not well within.

Changes in the Arab world

The **Arabs** also had their troubles. After the Suez-Sinai War in 1956 Nasser emerged as the most prominent figure in the Arab world. With the Soviet Union's help he had attempted to rebuild Egypt's military power and was largely responsible for the coming together of Egypt and Syria and the formation of the United Arab Republic (UAR).

The two countries hoped that shared interests would allow them to unite under a single government, but splits soon emerged with many in Syria, especially the military, feeling that the UAR parliament was dominated by Egyptians. The UAR collapsed after two years, shattering Nasser's dream of Arab unity, but the two continued to be united by one important thing – a hatred of the Israelis.

Elsewhere in the Arab world there was political turmoil. A new political group, the Ba'ath Party, had emerged to threaten established governments. Its policies were a mixture of **Communism** and Arab **Nationalism**, centred on anti-Israeli feelings. In Iraq it took over from the military dictator General Kassem in 1963 but was soon replaced by another military dictatorship in the form of General Aref. Syria was also experiencing a hard fight for control between left-wing groupings, resulting in a victory for the Ba'ath Party, which seized power in 1966.

Tension mounts

In 1964 the **Palestinian Liberation Organisation (PLO)** had been formed, replacing the **Fedayeen**. It began a bombing campaign in Israel. Buildings close to the **Knesset**, the Israeli parliament house, were destroyed and bombs exploded among football crowds. The PLO attacks came mainly from bases in Syria, now allied with Egypt, and Israel countered with attacks deep into Syrian territory. Syrian guns maintained a constant rain of attacks on Northern Israel, shelling Israeli settlements from the Golan Heights. In April 1967 the Israelis exacted revenge, bombing the Syrian guns before flying on to the capital Damascus in a clear show of strength.

Prelude to war

The tension was increased by Russian intelligence warnings that Israel intended to launch a full-scale attack against Syria. Nasser came under pressure to show leadership, condemned by both Syria and Jordan for his lack of action. On 16 May he made his intentions clear, ordering the withdrawal of UNEF (**United Nations** Emergency Force) from the Sinai Peninsula. This UN force had patrolled the area since the 1956 war, acting as a buffer between Egypt and Israel. Their departure was marked by the arrival of the Egyptian army. On 22 May, Nasser blocked the Gulf of Aqaba, a highly provocative action that effectively sealed off Israeli shipping from the Straits of Tiran. Israel interpreted this as a clear declaration of war and began to prepare accordingly. It was decided that Israel could not hope to fight a defensive war against several Arab states at once. Instead a lightning strike against Egypt and Syria was planned.

An Israeli column advances into Syria, June 1967.

An Egyptian jet destroyed before it could take off. The speed of Israel's attack stunned the Arab world.

Victory in six days

The war was a stunning success for the Israelis. It was effectively won on the day it began and it seemed as though Nasser had neither the time nor the tactical know-how to manage any kind of adequate response. The entire operation went like clockwork and was flawlessly executed.

5 June 1967

Israeli jets launched an early morning attack on Egyptian air bases. They completely wiped out the Egyptian air defences, destroying many planes before they could leave the ground. Later that day, in another round of attacks, they destroyed the Jordanian, Syrian and Iraqi Air Forces. Things were now nicely in place for Israeli land forces to sweep with ease over the Sinai Desert. In a mere six days Egyptian troops had been forced back to the Suez Canal. Jerusalem and the West Bank were captured and Israel seized the Golan Heights. By 10 June it was all over. It had been swift, ruthless and expertly executed. The capture of Jerusalem was especially pleasing to the Israelis, leading Moshe Dayan, the Israeli Defence Minister to declare: 'We have returned home to this most sacred of shrines never to part from it again.'

Immediate after effects

Arab prestige had been shattered by the nature of their defeat, while the Israelis were in a stronger position than ever before. They refused to withdraw from their newly acquired territories, the Golan Heights, Sinai, the West Bank of the River Jordan and the Gaza Strip. Conflict with Egypt continued in the Sinai area, but Israel's security was greatly increased. The **Palestinians** in the West Bank and Gaza found themselves back under Israeli control. To many of the refugees it was now clear that they could not rely on the Arab states to defeat Israel. Instead they would turn to the **PLO** as their only chance of liberation.

'. . . no peace with Israel, no recognition of Israel, no negotiations with it, and insistence on the rights of the Palestinian people in their own country.'
An extract from the Khartoum Declaration of 1 September 1967, in which the leaders of the Arab states affirmed their unity after the Six-Day War

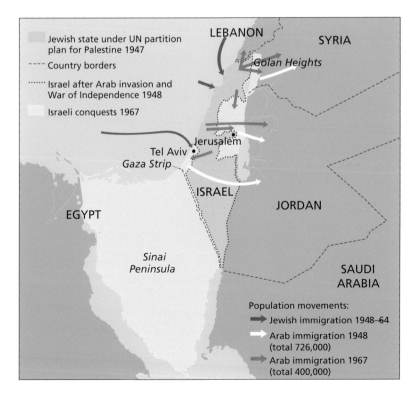

Jewish state under UN partition plan for Palestine 1947

---- Country borders

.... Israel after Arab invasion and War of Independence 1948

Israeli conquests 1967

Population movements:
➡ Jewish immigration 1948–64
➡ Arab immigration 1948 (total 726,000)
➡ Arab immigration 1967 (total 400,000)

LEBANON
SYRIA
Golan Heights
Jerusalem
Tel Aviv
Gaza Strip
ISRAEL
JORDAN
EGYPT
Sinai Peninsula
SAUDI ARABIA

The map shows the changing face of the Middle East since the Second World War.

Turning Point: Yom Kippur

In the years after the Six-Day War there was continued fighting in Sinai between Israeli and Egyptian forces. Nasser hoped to slowly wear down the Israelis, forcing them to withdraw. The new Prime Minister of Israel, Golda Meir, retaliated, launching air strikes deep into Egyptian territory. Nasser was alarmed and sought help from the Soviet Union who provided modern weapons in return for the use of Egyptian air and naval facilities. This placed the United States in a difficult position. Although supportive of Israel, they could not risk being dragged into a conflict in the Middle East that might involve the Soviet Union. American pressure forced Meir to call off the raids and enter into negotiations with Egypt in 1970.

Golda Meir addressing the world's press in London 1970.

Anwar Sadat

During these negotiations President Nasser died, and was replaced by his deputy, Anwar Sadat. He was willing to negotiate with both the United States and Israel, feeling that this was the best way to achieve the Egyptian goal of an Israeli withdrawal from Sinai. Meir, on the other hand, felt that Israel's security depended on Sinai and was unwilling to trade territory. In the years that followed Sadat began to believe that only war would bring Israel to the negotiating table.

War plans

Sadat knew that he could not risk war without the support of other **Arab** leaders, so entered into talks with the new leader of Syria, President Assad. Syria also had a grudge against the Israelis and hoped to regain the Golan Heights which it had lost in the 1967 war. The friendship between the two leaders was soon clear.

Israel ignored the warning signs, still confident of its own military strength after the easy victory of 1967. A complacent attitude prevailed in Israel, with many in the military regarding Arab forces as weak and disorganized. President Sadat was happy to encourage these feelings, emphasizing the poor condition of his army to western journalists.

Yom Kippur

The Israelis were shaken out of their complacency when Egyptian and Syrian forces launched surprise attacks on 6 October 1973. The day was Yom Kippur, an important **Jewish** religious festival. Many soldiers were home on leave, weakening the Israeli defences along the Suez Canal and in the Golan Heights. Egyptian tanks were able to overwhelm the Israeli forces and advance across the canal.

Weapons supplied by the USSR were crucial to the early Egyptian successes. When the Israeli airforce tried to strike back, they were met with a barrage of Soviet-made ground-to-air missiles. In the north, the Syrians attacked with over a thousand tanks advancing into the Golan Heights.

Early Arab successes, however, could not be maintained. Israel was able to quickly move men, tanks and equipment into Sinai and hit back at the Egyptians. On 14 October 1973 the two nations fought the biggest tank battle of the 20th century in the Sinai desert. Over 250 Egyptian tanks were destroyed, against only ten Israeli, allowing the Israelis to advance over the Suez Canal and threaten to encircle the Egyptian Third Army. Soviet spy satellites were able to detect this move and Sadat hastily began negotiations towards a **ceasefire**. When the ceasefire was called on 22 October it was swiftly broken by the Israelis who hoped to finish off the Third Army. The threat of full-scale Soviet involvement and pressure from the United States, however, forced an end to the conflict.

Results of the war

The Yom Kippur War showed clearly the central role played by both **superpowers** in the Middle East. The United States and USSR supplied the weaponry which enabled Egypt and Israel to fight battles on a massive scale. Both superpowers were anxious to end the conflict, America fearing a Soviet invasion, the Soviets recognizing that their ally, Egypt, faced defeat. The level of involvement was clearly illustrated when the US went on a full nuclear alert, the highest stage of war readiness, when it heard of the Soviet threat to invade. This forced the USSR to drop its threat.

The oil weapon

Arab nations used their immense supplies of oil as a weapon and a bargaining chip to great advantage during the conflict. The Organization of the Petroleum Exporting Countries (OPEC) forced the price of oil up by over 70 per cent and production was slowly reduced, threatening to starve the west of oil. Later in the year they raised prices by over 100 per cent, forcing the west, in particular Britain and the United States, to adopt less pro-Israeli policies. Pressure from the west forced Israel to 'disengage' from the Egyptian forces. They pulled back from their post-**ceasefire** positions and were replaced by **United Nations** troops. Realizing the potential of the oil weapon, the Arab nations began to show a new self-confidence in their dealings with Israel and the west.

Henry Kissinger, the US Secretarey of State, arrives in Israel in October 1973. Superpower pressure was crucial to bringing the Yom Kippur conflict to an end.

Superpower involvement and the use of OPEC's 'oil weapon' pressured Israel into taking part in peace talks with its Arab neighbours, eventually resulting in the Camp David Agreement (see page 32–35).

The Yom Kippur War, although ultimately a military defeat for the Arabs, restored much of the pride that the Egyptians had lost during the 1967 war. President Assad of Syria announced soon after: '... *in those days of heroism, we corrected many mistaken ideas which were established about our nations. We have restored self-confidence to the Arab and we have proved to the enemy that our people are not the easy prey that the enemy thought.*'

Motorists in Britain queue for petrol in the 1973 fuel crisis following the Arab OPEC nations' use of oil as a bargaining tool in the conflict.

Turning Point: Camp David

The years following the Yom Kippur War of 1973 saw great changes in Middle Eastern politics. By 1977 Israel was in economic turmoil, with high inflation and political scandals rocking the left-wing Mapai government of Yitzhak Rabin.

In May 1977 the right wing Likud (Unity) Party of Menachem Begin won most seats in a general election. Begin had been leader of the Irgun, a **Jewish guerrilla** group that had committed atrocities against **Arabs** during the 1948 war. With Begin in charge, a peace settlement seemed unlikely.

Pressure mounts

In 1976 Jimmy Carter replaced Gerald Ford as President of the United States. He immediately made it clear that peace in the Middle East was an important priority. He met with the Syrian leader, President Assad, in an attempt to encourage him to help negotiate a peace settlement that would settle the major issues of the region – the Golan Heights, Sinai, the West Bank and a homeland for the **Palestinians**. Assad, however, was keen that Palestinian areas should become part of Syria so was unwilling to push for such a deal. Begin also seemed unlikely to support it, instead encouraging Jewish settlement of the West Bank.

The situation appeared deadlocked, but President Sadat was anxious that Egypt, not Syria, should show a lead to the Arab world. In November 1977 he offered to become the first Arab leader to travel to Israel for talks. Although suspicious, Begin could not afford to risk angering the United States so was willing to accept the offer.

Sadat in the Knesset

On 20 November President Sadat made an historic speech in the **Knesset**, the Israeli parliament. He offered a peace agreement between Israel and Egypt which would deal with the land gained by Israel in the 1967 war and the issue of a Palestinian homeland. Other Arab nations were furious. In travelling to Israel Sadat had given recognition to the existence of the state of Israel. He was now offering a separate peace deal which would undermine Arab unity.

Camp David

In July 1978 Begin and Sadat met with President Carter at Camp David in the US state of Maryland. Secret talks followed, aimed at solving the problems of Israel's occupation of Sinai and the West Bank. Two documents emerged. In 'The Framework for a Peace Treaty' Israel agreed to return Sinai to Egyptian control over a three-year period in return for the Egyptians reopening the Suez Canal and Straits of Tiran to Israeli shipping. In the second document, 'The Framework for Peace', Begin agreed to hold talks about the future of Gaza and the West Bank, aimed at some form of Palestinian self-government within five years. The second framework was very vague, Egypt was in no position to negotiate on behalf of the Palestinians or other Arab states, and in the end nothing came of its proposals.

Profile: Anwar Sadat 1918–1981

Anwar Sadat came from a peasant background but he was able to rise to become an army officer. His intense hatred of British involvement in Egypt led to his being imprisoned for links with the Nazis during the Second World War. He returned to the army in 1950 and joined in Nasser's revolt, overthrowing the corrupt regime of King Farouk. He held a variety of posts in Nasser's government, before succeeding him as President of Egypt in 1970. After Egypt's failure in the Yom Kippur War he lessened the country's dependence on the USSR and began to co-operate more with the United States. In 1977 he bravely visited Israel, pressurizing the Israeli Prime Minister, Menachem Begin, into taking part in the Camp David peace talks. This move, and his more pro-western approach, led to attacks from other Arab nations and militant Islamic groups in Egypt. This resulted in his assassination in 1981.

Camp David, September 1978. President Sadat of Egypt (left) and Israeli Prime Minister, Menachem Begin make a historic handshake, with US President Jimmy Carter looking on.

Results of Camp David

On his return from the United States, Begin successfully persuaded the **Knesset** to withdraw Israeli troops and settlers from the Sinai Peninsula, making a peace treaty possible. The two leaders returned to Camp David, signing an historic peace treaty on 26 March 1979.

The Camp David Agreement was the first peace treaty signed between Israel and an **Arab** state, bringing an end to thirty years of conflict with Egypt. Israel began to withdraw from Sinai in May 1979, completing its withdrawal in 1982, and Begin and Sadat were awarded the Nobel Peace prize.

Arab countries, however, were furious. In signing a separate peace treaty, Sadat had weakened the position of other Arab states that still aimed for the destruction of Israel. His opposition to **Islamic Fundamentalist** groups both inside and outside Egypt placed him under greater pressure. On 6 October 1981, attending a parade to mark the anniversary of the Yom Kippur War, Sadat was assassinated by members of an extremist group.

Paying the price

In signing the Camp David agreement Sadat not only helped bring peace between Egypt and Israel, he also effectively signed his own death warrant. Soon after the agreement the Syrian government proclaimed:

'He (Sadat) shed all respect when he stood in Jerusalem and saluted the Israeli flag and leaders and bowed . . . Sadat is a cheap example of treachery . . . (his) end will be like other traitors.'

Two years later he was assassinated.

Profile: Menachem Begin (1913–1992)

Originally from Russia, Begin became involved in **Zionist** youth movements at the age of 16. After spending time in concentration camps in the Soviet Union, Begin was able to escape to Palestine where he assumed command of the Irgun in 1943. He was to play a major role in the struggle for independence both before and after the British withdrawal, including the attack on Deir Yassin in 1948.

After Israel gained independence Begin formed the Herut (Freedom) party and was elected to Israel's parliament, the Knesset. The Herut, which later combined with other right-wing parties to form the Likud (Unity) group, adopted a strongly **nationalist** line, advocating seizing further territory on both banks of the river Jordan. During the Six-Day War his hard-line views became more acceptable, eventually allowing him to become Prime Minister in 1977. He became the first Israeli leader to meet with the head of an Arab State that year as he began talks with Anwar Sadat. The resulting Camp David Accords led to the two being awarded the Nobel Peace prize. Nevertheless he was still prepared to take strong action to defend Israel and authorized the invasion of the Lebanon in 1982, before standing down as Prime Minister in 1983.

Menachem Begin, Prime Minister of Israel until 1983.

Turning Point: War in the Lebanon

The Lebanon, a small country to the north of Israel, became independent in 1945. Its people were divided fairly evenly between **Muslims** and Christians until the 1948 war brought 100,000 **Palestinian** refugees into the country. By 1970 this figure had risen to 300,000, a tenth of the country's population. Each new phase of the **Arab**-Israeli conflict created division between Muslims and Christians in the country, threatening its new found prosperity.

The arrival of the PLO

The Six-Day War of 1967 drove thousands of Palestinian refugees out of the West Bank area, many making their way to the Lebanon. Along with the refugees came members of the **PLO** who, from 1968 onwards, began using the Lebanon as a base for launching attacks on Israel. This situation worsened in late 1970 when King Hussein expelled the PLO from Jordan. The PLO set up its new headquarters in the Lebanon, making it increasingly difficult for the Lebanese army to limit PLO operations. The **Fedayeen** assaults into Israel increased, resulting in Israeli **reprisals** in the Lebanon in the form of air strikes and commando raids. The fragile peace between Lebanese Christians and Muslims was stretched to breaking point.

Beirut, 28 August 1982. A young PLO fighter is seen off by Yasser Arafat as the PLO begin their withdrawal from the Lebanon.

Israeli artillery on the attack in south Lebanon.

Civil war

The arrival of the PLO had heightened tension in the Lebanon and its decision to support the Muslim groups hastened the outbreak of a civil war. From 1975 Christian groups such as the Phalangist and Tiger **militias** fought Shi'ite and Druze Muslim militias, who were allied with the PLO. 40,000 people died and large areas of Beirut, the once prosperous capital, were destroyed. It was unlikely that the Lebanon's two powerful neighbours, Israel and Syria, would sit idly by and watch as the country disintegrated. The Syrians regarded the Lebanon as part of their territory and were concerned that the PLO and Muslim militias were becoming too powerful. Israel hoped to maintain a useful ally in a Christian Lebanese government. Syria was first to intervene, first working to subdue the PLO and Muslims, then turning on the Christian militias.

Israel intervenes

Palestinian **guerrillas** staging raids on Israel from Lebanese territory in turn drew Israeli raids on Lebanon, as well as two large-scale Israeli invasions. In March 1978 the Israelis invaded south Lebanon in an attempt to create a **'buffer zone'** to lessen the impact of PLO attacks. They withdrew in June after the **UN** Security Council created a 6000-man peacekeeping force for the area, called UNIFIL. As they departed, the Israelis turned over their strong points in the south, designed to help prevent PLO attacks across the border, to a Christian militia that they had organized, instead of to the UN force.

The second Israeli invasion came on 6 June 1982 after an assassination attempt by Palestinian terrorists on the Israeli ambassador in London. 172,000 heavily armed troops advanced deep into Lebanese territory, launching air strikes against PLO strongholds in residential areas of Beirut. They began to pull back their forces after a US envoy successfully negotiated the dispersal of most of the PLO to other Arab nations.

Massacre at Sabra-Chatila

The violence seemed to have come to an end when, on 14 September, Bashir Gemayel, the 34-year-old President-elect, was killed by a bomb that destroyed the headquarters of his Christian Phalangist Party. The day after the assassination, Israeli troops moved into West Beirut in force. They surrounded the Sabra-Chatila refugee camps, claiming that **PLO guerrillas** were using them as cover. In September 1982 the Israelis had allowed Christian militiamen to search the camps, resulting in the massacre of **Palestinians** in two refugee camps. Israel denied responsibility, but the massacre resulted in many Israelis turning against the war. The effects and repercussions of these events are discussed on pages 45 and 46.

Israel withdraws

Israeli forces began to withdraw their forces in 1983 and were replaced by a multinational peacekeeping force composed of US Marines and British, French, and Italian soldiers. Their mandate was to support the central Lebanese government, but they soon found themselves drawn into the struggle for power between different Lebanese factions. During their stay in Lebanon, 260 US Marines and about 60 French soldiers were killed, most of them in suicide bombings of the Marine and French army compounds on 23 October 1983. The multinational force left in the spring of 1984. The retreating Israeli forces also came under attack from Shi'ite suicide bombs. They eventually left the Lebanon in 1985, although they maintained a presence in the south to provide Israel with a 'security zone'.

US Marines search for the victims of the suicide bombing on their base in Beirut.

Continued conflict

The withdrawal of the bulk of Israel's forces did not bring peace to the Lebanon. In July 1986, Syrian observers took position in Beirut to monitor a peacekeeping agreement. The agreement soon broke down and fighting between Shi'ite and Druze **militia** in West Beirut became so intense that Syrian troops moved in in force in February 1987, suppressing militia resistance. Hostage taking of American and British **citizens** became commonplace, as **Muslim** militias tried to highlight their grievances. Meanwhile the PLO continued to make raids across the border into Israel. They were joined by a new extremist group, Hezbollah (Party of God), who were supported by Iran and Syria. Meanwhile, Christian forces, especially those led by General Michael Aoun, continued their 'war of liberation' against Syria.

Search for a settlement

The beginning of the end of the war came when Lebanon's leaders met in Ta'if, Saudi Arabia, in October 1989. There they formulated the Ta'if Agreement for a National Reconciliation Charter, which was approved on 4 November. A new President, René Moawad, was elected but was assassinated only 17 days later. His replacement Elias Hrawi, put down the rebellion of his fellow Christian General Aoun who was forced to flee to France. The fighting over, the new Government of National Reconciliation began the delicate task of disarming the militias and restoring stability. In a decade and a half of war, an estimated 130,000 to 150,000 people were killed and thousands more wounded.

Although the civil war had been brought to an end, some militia groups remained active. The Christian South Lebanese Army (SLA) refused to disband and Hezbollah continued to attack Israeli territory. As a result Israel refused to withdraw from southern Lebanon and launched **reprisal** attacks against Hezbollah strongholds throughout the 1990s. In 1996 the United States negotiated a truce whereby Hezbollah agreed not to attack Israeli territory but it was accepted that they could resist the Israeli forces in the 'security zone'. This, along with the eventual collapse of their Christian allies the SLA, forced the Israelis to act. In March 2000 the **Knesset** voted to withdraw all Israeli forces in southern Lebanon, with the last troops leaving on 24 May. The following day the Lebanese government declared an annual public holiday to be called 'Resistance and Liberation Day'.

A Global Conflict

The conflict between Israel and its **Arab** neighbours in the 1960s and 70s saw the emergence of many **guerrilla** and **militia** groups. While making peace with Egypt, the Israelis found themselves under attack from Fatah, the armed wing of the **PLO**. Fatah operated from the West Bank area, Jordan and the Lebanon, carrying out bombings in Israel itself and engaging in gun battles with Israeli troops. Between 1967 and 1970, Fatah attacks claimed the lives of more Israeli troops than had been killed in the Six-Day War: over 500, as well as 116 **civilians**.

However, throughout the 1970s it became clear to many **Palestinian** supporters that they could neither hope to defeat the Israelis themselves nor rely on Arab states to do it for them. While some Arab states, particularly Egypt, seemed to be coming to terms with their Israeli neighbours, some Palestinians felt that their cause was being sidelined.

The extension of the conflict

In the early 1970s new Palestinian groups emerged, determined that world opinion would not forget about their cause. These new groups, such as the Popular Front for the Liberation of Palestine (PFLP) and Black September, were prepared to use more extreme methods.

The PFLP organized a series of aircraft hijacks which resulted in many deaths but attracted the attention of the world's media. In one of their most spectacular attacks, three airliners were forced to fly to an airstrip in Jordan. Six hundred passengers were held hostage with the PFLP demanding the release from prison of one of their members. When the British government released the hijacker, the passengers were freed before the three planes were blown apart in full view of the world's press.

Black September

The PFLP hijack forced King Hussein of Jordan to take action against the PLO in his own country. In September 1970 the Jordanian army expelled the PLO, forcing them to retreat into Syria and the Lebanon. Palestinians called the expulsion 'Black September', a name adopted by a new guerrilla group. In 1971 they assassinated the Prime Minister of Jordan in a clear revenge attack for events of the previous year. The following year Black September carried out their most infamous action. They kidnapped eleven Israeli athletes who were taking part in the

The Olympic flag flies at half mast as crowds attend a memorial service for the Israeli athletes killed by Arab terrorists.

1972 Munich Olympics in Germany. A gun battle with police followed in which all eleven hostages were killed, as well as five members of Black September. World public opinion was shocked by the attack – the Olympic Games were regarded as a beacon of peace, free from politics – but again the Palestinian cause was front-page news.

Raid on Entebbe

In the late 1970s Palestinian groups began to move away from hijacking as a means of attracting publicity. This is partly explained by the events which followed a hijacking in 1976. Four terrorists had ordered a plane carrying over 200 passengers from Israel to France to instead land at Entebbe in Uganda. The 110 Israeli passengers on board were held hostage, with the terrorists demanding that 53 Palestinians should be released from jails in Europe and Israel. Instead of meeting their demands the Israelis flew a group of commandoes 2500 miles to Uganda. Under cover of darkness they burst into the airport building and killed all the terrorists, taking just 45 seconds to carry out their mission. It was now clear to terrorists backing the Palestinians that Israel was prepared to go to great lengths to defend its people.

America becomes a target

The decline in hijacking, however, was only a change in tactics, rather than an end to terrorist attacks. The 1982 invasion of the Lebanon led to the rise of other groups determined to strike back at Israel and its allies. Increasingly, some **fundamentalist Islamic** states, such as Iran and Libya, began to regard the United States as an enemy of the **Arab** people. To such states the US was the main ally of Israel, its main source of weapons and diplomatic support in the **UN**. The targeting of American troops and **civilians** became common as Arab groups tried to publicize their cause and force a change in US government policy.

In 1983 a Shi'ite **militia** called Amal was set up in the Lebanon, intent on forcing the Israelis and the US peacekeepers out of the country. Later in the year another suicide bomber drove into the US Marine base. In the resulting explosion 219 people were killed and 75 injured. In February 1984, President Reagan ordered a withdrawal, but the US has remained a target for Islamic fundamentalists. This was never clearer than on 11 September 2001 when suicide bombers loyal to terrorist leader Osama bin Laden crashed passenger jets into both towers of the World Trade Center and the Pentagon, killing many thousands of people. President George W Bush declared war on bin Laden and terrorism.

Crash investigators in Lockerbie search for evidence around the remains of the cockpit of Pan Am flight 103, 23 December 1988.

Libya and the United States

In 1969 a group of army officers led by Colonel Qaddafi seized power in the north African state of Libya. Qaddafi was a devout follower of Islam and hoped that he and his country could play a dominant role in Arab affairs.

He soon made his hatred of the western powers clear, offering support to terrorist groups willing to strike at countries such as the United States and Britain. Money and weapons were provided for groups such as the **PLO** and the IRA (Irish Republican Army), and soon a diverse range of left-wing and Islamic terrorist groups were looking to Qaddafi for support.

The regime was believed to be linked to a series of assassinations and terrorist activities. Tensions between Libya and the United States were raised in 1981 when US Navy jets shot down two Libyan planes. In 1986, responding to heightened terrorism apparently directed by Libya against Americans in Europe, the US bombed sites in Libya declared by President Ronald Reagan to be 'terrorist centres' including Tripoli. Several dozen Libyans died in the attack, including Qaddafi's two-year-old adopted daughter.

Two years later Arab bombers struck. 270 people died when Pan Am flight 103 was blown out of the sky over Lockerbie, Scotland on 21 December 1988. It was the worst ever act of airline terrorism against the United States. It has also been called the world's biggest unsolved murder.

Although some observers believe that Syria or Iran were involved, the US accused Libya of harbouring the bombers. In 1992 the UN introduced **sanctions** against Libya and a prolonged campaign for their **extradition** has followed. After extensive negotiations Qaddafi conceded that the two suspects could be put on trial in the Netherlands, a neutral venue, in May 2000. America, however, remains a target for Arab extremists.

The Media and the Conflict

The media, both within the Middle East and around the globe, has had an important role to play in the fifty years of tension and war between Israel and her neighbours. Inevitably over the past fifty years there have been many changes in the media's perception of the conflict. The importance of the region has ensured that the international media has kept a close eye on political developments, while in Israel and the **Arab** states the media has been central to the promotion of both peace and war.

Lebanese women fighting Israeli soldiers at Ramallah, 1988. Images like these helped to turn world opinion about Israel's position in the Lebanon.

Early years of the conflict

The state of Israel was born in the turbulent years that followed the Second World War. In Britain the public yearned for peace so stories of British soldiers dying in Palestine soon forced the government to hand over control of the area to the **UN**. Images of the Nazi **Holocaust** were still fresh in the minds of many in the West and public sympathy was very much with the **Jews**. Images of Jewish refugees being turned away by British warships as they approached Palestine shocked the world.

The propaganda effect of the ships decked with British flags daubed with Nazi Swastikas forced a change in government policy, allowing more Jewish refugees into Palestine. The media had been central to the creation of Israel and would later play an important role in forcing a British climb down during the Suez Crisis. The importance of the media in shaping world opinion and the government policies towards the Middle East was clear.

The media's role in the Six-Day War 1967

In the build up to the Six-Day War the media in some Arab states helped whip their readers and listeners into frenzy, encouraging them to expect a swift and glorious victory. Cartoons in Egyptian and Lebanese newspapers portrayed Israel as a weak nation surrounded by more powerful Arab enemies. In May Cairo Radio declared: 'It is our chance, Arabs, to direct a blow of death and annihilation to Israel and all its presence in our Holy Land'. The defeat that followed stunned the Arab world, and its media was forced to accept its role in raising expectations. The Egyptian magazine *Al-Mussawar* admitted encouraging Egypt's government to adopt an aggressive position: 'We have been saying things that we did not always mean ... its main influence was on the Arabs; it raised their expectations to a point where promises had to be fulfilled'.

Israel's first defeat: the Lebanon

Until the 1982 invasion of the Lebanon the Israeli media had generally been supportive of the government's strong line with its Arab neighbours. The world's press, while concerned at the on-going conflict, had also broadly accepted the view that it was Arab states, not Israel, that were the aggressors in the region. Events in the Lebanon changed that perception, and Israel found itself under fire both at home and abroad.

The massacre of **Palestinian** refugees in the Sabra-Chatila camps stunned the world. The Israeli government tried to wash its hands of the crime, blaming the Christian Phalangists. Menachem Begin made his government's position clear: 'Non-Jews kill non-Jews – and the world wants to hang Israel for the crime'. Advertisements were taken out in the American press claiming that the Israeli army could have done nothing to prevent the massacres.

Criticism nevertheless grew: although the Israeli army had not taken part, they had stood by as their allies carried out the killings, in some cases within earshot of the cries of the victims. For the first time the Israeli press began to criticize government defence policy. One journalist, comparing the massacres to Nazi atrocities committed against the **Jews**, wrote: 'We shall never be able to cleanse ourselves of this stain'.

Media pressure at home and abroad grew and 400,000 people took part in an anti-war demonstration in Tel Aviv. Israeli Defence Minister, Ariel Sharon, resigned and Israel was forced to withdraw from the country the following year. Media pressure had again influenced events in the region.

Global terrorism

The pro-**Palestinian** and **Islamic fundamentalist** terror groups that emerged in the 1970s were keen to exploit the media to promote their cause. After the hijack of three aircraft in 1970 the leader of the PFLP, George Habash, made clear the importance of attracting media attention: 'For decades world public opinion has been neither for or against the Palestinians. At least the world is talking about us now.' The killing of eleven Israeli athletes in 1972 achieved the same goal. Later Lebanese Islamic groups adopted a new tactic. Western **civilians** working in Beirut were taken hostage and held for long periods in terrible conditions, their plight highlighting the cause of the kidnappers. However, the publicity generated by such actions, while gaining exposure, did little to attract international sympathy to the **Arab** cause.

Terry Waite, the Archbishop of Canterbury's envoy was kidnapped by Shi'ite Muslims in 1987, and held hostage in Beirut until 1991.

In the United States in particular some Arab nations, notably Libya, and terrorist groups have become the cause of much popular fear and hatred. Since the collapse of the Soviet Union fear of nuclear attack from 'rogue Arab states' has replaced the **communist** threat. Following the attacks of 11 September 2001, this fear has focussed on the terrorist leader Osama bin Laden. The US media has been heavily committed to the support of Israel, forcing politicians to adopt a similar attitude or risk attack from the press.

The *Los Angeles Times*, 15 April 1986. The US media was strongly supportive of President Reagan's retaliation for an earlier bombing in which an American serviceman was killed.

The Intifada

It was not until 1987 that a new Palestinian movement was able to attract widespread public sympathy. When the young people of the West Bank rose up in the **Intifada** Israel did not know how to react. It was difficult to denounce such a popular and uncoordinated movement as the work of 'terrorists'. Despite the hard-line 'iron-fist' policy, in which he famously advised the security forces to 'break the bones of the rioters' they detained, Defence Minister Yitzhak Rabin prevailed. However, with every televised incident of Israel's heavy-handed response, the Palestinians rose in international stature while the Israelis lost more and more credibility. The casualties were high. Some 1300 Palestinians, including 300 children, were killed, but the popular unrest and its coverage had stunned the international community. The need for a permanent solution appeared more important than ever.

The international media had again played an important role in pressing for a peaceful solution to the conflict. The images of the Intifada were a crucial factor in pushing the Israeli government into engaging in peace talks, as well as allowing the **PLO** to gain publicity without the need for terrorist type attacks.

Turning Point: Hopes for Peace

On 9 December 1987, the **Intifada** (Arabic for 'Uprising') erupted. This outbreak of violence, with images of confrontations between stone-throwing **Arab** youths and the Israeli army flashing around the world, helped lead to the fragile peace process in the Middle East during the 1990s.

The Intifada. Images of poorly equipped Palestinian youths clashing with the Israeli army shocked the world.

The Intifada

The first demonstrations and clashes were not the responsibility of the **PLO** but were a response to the continued Israeli occupation of Gaza and the West Bank. Militant religious groups such as **Islamic** Jihad and Hamas, helped turn this frustration into direct action.

The spread of the rebellion into Israel itself alarmed the Israelis. The reaction of the Israeli army was swift and decisive. Yitzhak Rabin (Defence Minister in the **coalition** government) announced an 'iron-fist' policy, ordering his soldiers to use live ammunition against the rioters. However, the violence of the army was counter-productive. Their actions, broadcast on news bulletins around the world, brought international condemnation.

Usually a reliable ally of Israel, the United States joined in the criticism. Israeli Prime Minister Yitzhak Shamir refused to be swayed by international opinion but it was becoming clear that efforts to end the unrest using the military were failing.

Some form of **Palestinian** self-rule seemed the only possible solution. US Secretary of State George Schultz set out a peace plan in February 1988. Foreign Minister Shimon Peres, leader of the Labour Party in the governing coalition, backed the plan but Shamir remained firmly opposed along with the majority of Israel's **Jewish** population. The plan stalled and the Intifada intensified.

PLO recognizes Israel

Attention now turned to the question of whether the PLO, as the representative of the Palestinian people, was prepared to recognize the state of Israel. The Palestinian National Charter of July 1968 had declared Palestine to be their homeland and had called for armed struggle to secure the 'elimination of **Zionism** in Palestine'. This objective, translated in many minds as 'the destruction of Israel', seemed to be confirmed by the actions of the PLO in the years that followed. Why should the PLO now change its mind?

The effects of the Intifada

The Intifada had not only placed the issue of the Middle East in the forefront of world attention, it had also aroused a wave of international sympathy for the Palestinian cause along with a feeling that something should be done. However, as the Intifada had shown, Israel could not be removed from the **Occupied Territories** by Palestinian action alone. Israel had a firm policy of refusing to talk with the PLO, which it regarded as a terrorist organization. For the Palestinians to make any progress, it was necessary to enlist the aid of the world's major powers. The Soviet Union was preoccupied with its own internal problems so it was to the west, and principally the USA, that the Palestinians had to turn if they wanted assistance.

The Americans however had promised that they would not talk to the PLO until it had recognized the state of Israel and its right to exist, and renounced the use of terrorism.

Steps to recognition

Through the closing months of 1988 intense diplomatic activity led to a series of meetings as the **PLO** tried to make its policies more acceptable to the USA. The most notable steps were:

* 5 November – The **Palestinian** National Council declared a Palestinian state, with Jerusalem as its capital. It also proclaimed its acceptance of **UN** resolutions 242 and 338 that recognize Israel's right to exist.
* 13 December – Arafat spoke to the United Nations General Assembly in Geneva.
* 14 December – At a specially convened press conference Arafat affirmed Israel's right to exist in peace and security and added: 'We totally and absolutely renounce all forms of terrorism'.

Within four hours of this pronouncement American Secretary of State George Schultz announced that the USA would open negotiations with the PLO. The Israelis were furious.

The Gulf War

The Iraqi invasion of Kuwait in August 1990 was to prove crucial. The Iraqis found themselves under immense pressure to withdraw, but their leader, Saddam Hussein, steadfastly refused. He argued that if the UN demanded the withdrawal of his troops from Kuwait, they must do the same with Israeli forces in the Lebanon. The PLO announced that they backed Iraq, and there was sympathy in **Arab** nations. Despite this a US-led **coalition** launched an attack on 17 January 1991, backed by many Arab states. The war lasted only 43 days but would have long-lasting repercussions, kick starting the peace process.

Peace talks begin

The PLO's decision to support Iraq in the Gulf War of 1991 had been a diplomatic disaster. Many of the Gulf states who had supported the US coalition were also financial backers of the PLO. The threat of withdrawal of funding forced many in the PLO to adopt a more positive approach to talks with Israel. In November 1991 peace talks between the Israelis, Arab nations and the Palestinians were held in Madrid. Under the spotlight of the world's media little was achieved.

The Oslo Accords

In the 1992 Israeli elections, Yitzhak Rabin's Labour Party had defeated Shamir's right-wing coalition. Rabin, who had ordered the 'iron-fist' policy at the onset of the **Intifada**, had since realized that force could not subdue the uprising. He also recognized that the **Jewish** population of Israel would soon be surpassed by the substantially higher birth rate of the Palestinians. Arafat appeared to be leading the PLO towards more moderate policies so the time seemed right for negotiations.

From January 1993 secret talks were held in Oslo, eventually resulting in the Oslo Accords. On 13 September in Washington the agreement was formally signed by Rabin, Arafat and President Clinton, and appeared to offer fresh hope to the troubled region.

Israeli Prime Minister Yitzhak Rabin signs the Washington Agreement that formally ratifies the Oslo Accords. Behind him US President Bill Clinton and Yasser Arafat of the PLO look on.

The main terms of the Oslo Accords were:

- Israel would withdraw from the **Occupied Territories** of the Gaza Strip and Jericho, allowing the Palestinians to take over their administration. Soon after they would become responsible for the security of the two areas.
- Jewish settlers would remain in the territories, but would come under Israeli jurisdiction.
- After two years the negotiations would move on to a second phase, when issues such as the future of Jerusalem and Israeli settlements would be discussed.

A False Dawn?

The Oslo Accords and the historic handshake between Rabin and Arafat on the White House Lawn appeared to offer new hope for peace in the Middle East but obstacles remained. An angry reaction from extremists both within Israel and among the **Palestinians** has meant that negotiations after Oslo have taken place against a background of violence. Despite this, the Israelis and the **PLO** have tried to press on with the implementation of their plans.

Massacre at Hebron – end of the Intifada

The peace process seemed doomed early in 1994 when events in the West Bank town of Hebron threatened to shatter the fragile accord between Rabin and Arafat. The area around Hebron contained many **Jewish** settlers and one village, Kiryat Arba, had become a centre for Jewish extremism.

On 25 February an immigrant from New York, Dr Bernard Goldstein, entered the Tomb of the Patriarchs in Hebron, a holy site for both **Muslims** and Jews. He opened fire on a crowd of praying Muslims, killing 29 people before being overcome. His actions sparked Palestinian violence throughout the West Bank and security force **reprisals**, but he was hailed as a hero among right-wing Jewish groups.

Israeli settlers protest in the West Bank.

In spite of the growing unrest, Arafat and Rabin pressed on. In May 1994 they reached agreement in Cairo setting out the terms for Palestinian self-rule. Soon after, Israeli troops began to withdraw and the **Intifada** ground to a halt. Later that year a historic peace treaty was signed between Israel and Jordan, the first with an **Arab** state since the 1979 Camp David Agreement. Following Jordan's lead, other Arab states began to open up diplomatic relations with Israel.

Violence and assassination

The implementation of the Oslo Accords soon brought a further upsurge in violence as extremists on both sides put pressure on their leaders. A new Palestinian group – Hamas – had emerged in the **Occupied Territories** during the Intifada, unhappy with Arafat's increasingly moderate policies. In 1994 it began a bombing campaign in Israel and gained further publicity when it kidnapped and killed an Israeli soldier.

This murder coincided with the award of the Nobel Peace Prize to Rabin, Arafat and Peres and brought calls for tighter security from many in Israel. Rabin warned that if the Palestinians did not subdue Hamas, then further self-rule was out of the question. Arafat was placed in a difficult position. His leadership was increasingly questioned as the new **Palestinian National Authority** attempted to control Hamas while the Israelis expanded their settlements around Jerusalem.

Despite this pressure September 1995 saw an agreement to extend Palestinian self-rule, closely followed by elections in Gaza, Jericho and the West Bank. This was the final straw for some right-wing Israelis. Yitzhak Rabin had been bearing the brunt of their anger. Rallies around Israel had declared him a traitor and some rabbis had been calling for his death. On 4 November he was gunned down by a Jewish extremist after addressing 100,000 people at a peace rally in Tel Aviv.

Rabin's assassination called into question the survival of the Peace Process. Shimon Peres, his successor as Prime Minister did not hold the same respect among the more militant voters in Israel. Israeli support for the peace process would be severely tested in the November 1996 elections.

The election of Netanyahu

The 1996 Israeli General election took place in an atmosphere of rising tension. Shimon Peres moved the election to May in the hope that he could exploit the revulsion at the death of Rabin. However, a Hamas bombing campaign brought an increasing number of Israeli voters behind Benjamin Netanyahu's right-wing Likud Party. Netanyahu narrowly won the election, promising to improve security and adopt a strong line with the **Palestinians**. His right wing **coalition** included extreme **Orthodox** groups who were unlikely to accept movement in the peace process.

Netanyahu soon made his policies clear. The **Jewish** settlement programme was expanded and he refused to meet Arafat, who in turn came under increasing pressure as his moderate policies began to falter. In September 1996 Hamas violence intensified when Netanyahu authorized the archaeological excavation of an ancient tunnel close to the Dome of the Rock in Jerusalem, an important **Muslim** site. It seemed as if the peace process had again reached a dead end.

Profile: Yitzhak Rabin (1922–1995)

Rabin was born in Jerusalem during the time of the **British Mandate**, becoming a member of a **Haganah** commando unit during the Second World War. After a brief period of imprisonment under the British he fought in the 1948 War of Independence before rising rapidly through the ranks of the Israeli army to become its commander in 1964. In this position he led the army in the 1967 Six-Day War, becoming a national hero. In 1974 he replaced Golda Meir as leader of the Labour Party and became the first Israeli Prime Minister who had been born in

the new state. After electoral defeat in 1977 he held a number of coalition government positions until again becoming Prime Minister in 1992. His efforts to reach peace with the Palestinians led to the Oslo Accords in 1993 and the Nobel Peace Prize in 1994. The following year he was assassinated, robbing Israel of a forceful champion of peace.

The coffin of Yitzhak Rabin is carried to Mount Herzl cemetery, 6 November 1995.

The Hebron and Wye River agreements

Part of the agreement that resulted from the 1993 Oslo talks was that Israel and the Palestinians would meet again within two years to discuss key issues. Instead, under Netanyahu, little was achieved other than protracted negotiations over how to put the Oslo Accords into action. In the Hebron agreement of January 1997 the Israelis agreed to withdraw from 80 per cent of that city, leaving a substantial force to protect the 400 Jewish settlers. In October 1998 the Wye River Agreement saw the Israelis agree to withdraw from a further 13.1 per cent of the West Bank and to allow movement between the Gaza Strip and the other Palestinian areas, as well as releasing 2000 Palestinian prisoners. In return Arafat agreed to crack down on Hamas with advice from American security experts. Little had been achieved; to many Palestinians all of the **Occupied Territories** should be handed over, not a mere 13 per cent, while to right-wing Israelis Netanyahu was going too far.

Israeli Prime Minister Benjamin Netanyahu meets PLO leader Yasser Arafat for the first time, 4 September 1996. Despite such meetings the peace process slowed down after the assassination of Rabin.

The election of Ehud Barak and the Camp David talks

July 1999 saw the defeat of Netanyahu in an Israeli general election. His successor, Ehud Barak, led a left-of-centre group called the One Israel Coalition. As Israel's most decorated soldier it was felt that he might be more likely to win the support of hard-liners for a peace deal so when he met with Arafat at Camp David in July 2000 hopes were high. However, it soon became clear that neither side was going to be able to reach a compromise. Barak's fragile coalition in the **Knesset** would not allow movement on control of Jerusalem. Arafat meanwhile was unwilling to negotiate an agreement that avoided tackling the status of Jerusalem, fearing violence in the Palestinian territories. Despite both sides again stating their desire to achieve a settlement that would bring lasting peace to the Middle East the talks broke down.

Peace shattered

Doubts about the talks at Camp David and the uncertain status of Jerusalem were justified within a few months. In late September 2000 violence erupted in Gaza and the West Bank after Israel's right-wing opposition leader Ariel Sharon led a delegation from his party to the place in Jerusalem that **Jews** call Temple Mount. **Muslims** call the site Haram al-Sharif, or Noble Sanctuary. The control of this site, sacred to both religions, is a crucial flashpoint in the peace process.

Sharon's provocative visit ignited the passions on each side of the conflict. **Palestinian** crowds attacked Israeli security forces with stones and gunfire. The Israeli response was swift and deadly. Attacks by troops firing live ammunition and helicopter gunships left more than 100 Palestinians dead and wounded in the weeks of confrontation.

The years of peace talks seemed to have been forgotten as stories emerged of brutality on both sides. Two Israeli soldiers were beaten to death by a Palestinian mob in Ramallah on the West Bank. The Israeli army retaliated with rocket attacks on the city. Each side blamed the other for the violence.

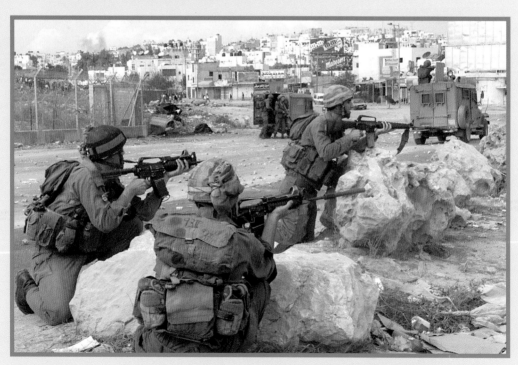

Fighting continues on the West Bank, 2000.

International fears

The international community was in no doubt that the fragile peace process had been shattered, possibly permanently, by the worst violence since 1996. The price of oil soared, an indication of the tension in the **Arab** world. The **United Nations** condemned Israel's attacks, which many felt were excessive, although the United States opposed the vote. There were signs that the conflict could spread across the Middle East when an American warship was attacked by Arab extremists in Yemen.

US President Bill Clinton and Egypt's President Mubarak attempted to broker a peace settlement but as the numbers of casualties rose, agreement became more unlikely. The election in February 2001 of a hard-line Israeli government led by Ariel Sharon, is likely to have a negative impact on the search for peace. Atrocities have continued on both sides.

On the Palestinian side, Yasser Arafat remains the dominant voice, as he has for so much of the conflict. As violence raged around him in the closing months of 2000 he remained both the most potent symbol of Palestinian defiance and possibly the only person who could bring the Palestinians back to the negotiating table with Israel.

A way forward?

Only 30 miles from the centre of the conflict in Jerusalem lies a community that may show a way forward for the people of the Middle East. The village of Neve Shalom, or New Peace, was set up in the 1970s. In this village, Jewish and Muslim families live together in the hope that their children will grow up as friends. However, even this small community cannot ignore the stresses of the world outside. Children have to attend all-Jewish or all-Arab schools in nearby towns and violence between Israel and the Palestinians makes life in the village difficult. As one resident says: 'Neve Shalom does not attempt to offer any solution to the Middle East peace process. We are simply living proof that it is possible for different groups to live together through very tough times, while maintaining our own separate identities.'

The Future

Without agreement on some unresolved key issues it is unlikely that any long lasting peace can be achieved in the Middle East.

1 A Palestinian state

In Oslo it was agreed that **Palestinians** living in the West Bank and Gaza could have a limited form of self-rule, with overall sovereignty lying with Israel. Palestinian hopes for their own sovereign state was left until later talks.

The final borders of the Palestinian state were also undecided. The Palestinians expect that state to comprise all of the Palestinian territories conquered in 1967. They argue that, in accepting the principle of statehood only in the West Bank and Gaza, they cannot be expected to compromise further. The Israelis accept a Palestinian state, but are concerned about their security. The larger the Palestinian area, the easier it would be for other **Arab** states to use it as a base to attack Israel.

2 Israeli settlements

Although the **Occupied Territories** never formally became part of Israel, tens of thousands of Israelis have settled on land taken from Palestinians. Today there are 155,000 Israeli settlers living in the West Bank and 6000 in Gaza.

The Palestinians argue that Israeli settlements are illegal, and that the settlers have to be removed under any peace agreement. However, they have been forced to accept that some settlers will remain in small areas guarded by the Israeli military. They remain flashpoints for violence between Israelis and Palestinians.

To the Israelis, the settlers are important especially as their towns and villages help provide a security presence throughout the West Bank. Right-wing groups in Israel would be furious if the settlers were 'betrayed', making compromise difficult.

Innocent civilians, like Sami Abu Jazar are caught in the fighting, 2000.

3 Jerusalem

The future of Jerusalem is one of the most emotional issues in the conflict and was a major sticking point in the Camp David talks. It is a holy site for both **Judaism** and **Islam**, but has been under Israeli control since the 1967 war.

The Palestinian position: The Palestinians call Jerusalem Al Quds and regard it as the capital of their future state. They want a divide between Israeli and Arab sections, with access to religious sites guaranteed.

The Israeli position: Israel insists that Jerusalem is its 'eternal' capital and that the city will remain undivided under its control, although they do concede access to religious sites.

4 Water

The shortage of water in the Middle East makes its allocation a central issue. A Water Resources Working Group was set up by the Oslo agreement. Israel, Jordan and the Palestinians were to try to work together to manage the demand for the region's diminishing water supplies.

The Palestinian position: Palestinians complain that many Palestinian houses are not connected to a water supply while Israeli settlers draw unlimited water from West Bank sources.

The Israeli position: Israel will not easily give up its control of West Bank water sources or access to the Jordan River. There have already been disputes with Jordan over the allocation of supplies from the Jordan River.

Hopes for compromise

As the violence continues in the West bank and Gaza, any settlement of the conflict seems unlikely, but there may be room for compromise. The issues of the Palestinian state and settlers have already seen movement from both sides while Israeli plans for an undersea water pipeline from Turkey may relieve tension over water supplies. The sticking point has been Jerusalem.

However, after fifty years of conflict there are reasons for hope. Two peoples, who at one stage swore to wipe each other from the face of the Earth, have engaged in negotiations, although decades of bitterness and the holiest city in the world stand in the way of a lasting settlement.

Appendix
Timeline

1914–1918 First World War, with Britain fighting alongside Arabs against Turkey

1917 Balfour Declaration: Britain agrees to support a Jewish homeland in Palestine

1920 Control of Palestine given to Britain under a League of Nations mandate.
Jewish immigrants in Palestine begin to increase.

1936 Arab Revolt against Britain begins

1939 Second World War begins.
Arab Revolt defeated.
Jewish immigration to Palestine is limited.

1944 Irgun terrorists begin attacks on British forces

1945 End of Second World War

1946 Irgun bombs King David Hotel, British military headquarters, Palestine

1947 Britain announces plans to leave Palestine.
UN decides to partition Palestine.

1948 British leave Palestine.
State of Israel declared.
Five Arab states invade Israel but are defeated, leaving thousands of Palestinian Arabs as refugees.

1952 Nasser becomes leader of Egypt

1955 Palestinian Fedayeen begin raids into Israel

1956 Suez-Sinai war: Israel conquers Sinai Peninsula but is forced to withdraw by UN the following year

1964 PLO set up

1967 Six-Day War: Israel conquers Sinai, the Gaza strip, the West Bank and the Golan Heights

1970 'Black September': King Hussein expels the PLO from Jordan.
Nasser dies; replaced by Sadat.

1972 Palestinians murder eleven Israeli athletes at the Munich Olympics

1973 Yom Kippur War.
First use of 'oil weapon' by Arab states.

1975 Civil war begins in Lebanon

1976 Israel rescues 100 hostages in the Entebbe raid

1977 Begin become Prime Minister of Israel.
Egyptian President Sadat visits Israel.

1978 Camp David peace deal between Israel and Egypt

1981 President Sadat assassinated

1982 Israelis withdraw from Sinai.
Israel invades the Lebanon.
PLO forced out of Beirut.
Christian militia members, watched by the Israelis, massacre Palestinian refugees in Sabra and Chatila camps.

1983 UN peacekeeping force arrives in the Lebanon.
260 US marines killed in a suicide bomb attack in Beirut.

1984 Peacekeeping force begins to leave Beirut

1985 Israel begins withdrawal from the Lebanon.
Kidnapping tactic introduced by fundamentalists in Beirut.

1986 United States bombs sites in Libya

1987 Palestinain Intifada begins in the Occupied Territories

1988 King Hussein cuts all Jordan's ties with West Bank.
PLO formally recognizes state of Israel.
Lockerbie bomb.

1989 Ta'if Agreement brings an end to war in the Lebanon

1990 Saddam Hussein's Iraq invades Kuwait; a US-led coalition is set up to oppose him

1991 Iraq defeated in the Gulf War.
Talks between Israelis and Palestinians begin.

1992 Yitzhak Rabin elected Israeli Prime Minister

1993 Oslo peace talks between Israel and PLO result in peace deal being signed in Washington.
Hamas violence intensifies.

1994 Hebron Massacre.
Palestinian self-rule begins.
End of the Intifada.
Israel and Jordan sign a peace deal.
Arafat, Rabin and Peres awarded Nobel Peace Prize.

1995 Yitzhak Rabin assassinated

1996 Palestinian self-rule elections held with Arafat winning a landslide victory.
Netanyahu defeats Peres in Israeli elections.

1997 Hebron agreement signed by Netanyahu and Arafat

1998 Wye River Agreement between Israel and Palestinians

1999 Ehud Barak defeats Netanyahu in Israeli general election

2000 Final Israeli withdrawal from the Lebanon.
Camp David talks fail to reach a final settlement.
September – October: Violence erupts across West Bank and Gaza with armed clashes between Palestinians and the Israeli army.

2001 *February*: Ariel Sharon elected Prime-Minister of Israel. Violence by Palestinians and Israeli army intensifies.
11 September: Attacks by Islamic terrorists destroy World Trade Center in New York. The conflict enters a new phase.

Suggested reading

Children of Israel, Children of Palestine : Our Own True Stories, by Laurel Holliday (Ed.) – Simon & Schuster Books 1999 (Stories from children caught in the conflict.)
The Arab Israeli Conflict, by T.G Fraser – MacMillan 1995
The Fifty Years War, Israel and the Arabs, by Bregman, El-Tahri – Penguin/BBC Books 1998

Useful websites

http://www.pmo.gov.il/english
 The Israeli government site
http://www.pna.net
 The Palestinian National Authority site
http://www.megastories.com/mideast
 A good site which explains the basics well
http://www.fresno.k12.ca.us/schools/s090/history/middle_east.htm
 A good site for background and links
http://www.dac.neu.edu/polisci/d.sullivan/peacequest.html
 An excellent explanatory site, many links

Glossary

anti-semitism actions or feelings of hatred toward Jewish people

Arab people who live in an area stretching from North Africa to the Middle East. Arabs are often, but not always, Muslims.

austere severe in attitude, especially regarding strict economic measures

British Mandate the period of British rule in Palestine after the First World War. Britain ran Palestine on behalf of the League of Nations.

buffer zones territory seized by Israel in order to force Arab countries to attack through non-Israeli areas, giving more time to prepare defences and reduce the impact of the attack on Israel itself

ceasefire a temporary truce in which time a permanent peace may be negotiated

citizen, citizenship a member of a society; citizenship brings rights and duties in a society

civilian a person who is not a member of the armed forces

coalition a temporary alliance, particularly of political parties in government

Cold War the state of hostility between Soviet powers and Western powers after the Second World War

communism, communist a political ideology that supports a classless society in which private ownership has been abolished

developed world the richer, industrial nations of the world

Diaspora the expulsion of the Jews from Palestine by the Romans in AD100

exile a long, usually enforced, absence from one's home or country

extradition handing over someone accused of a crime to the authorities of the country in which the crime was committed

Fedayeen an Arabic term meaning 'self sacrificers', used by Palestinians who carried out raids against Israel in the early years of the conflict

fundamentalist someone who believes in strictly following the rules of the Koran, the holy book of Islam

guerrilla a soldier who prefers tactics such as ambushes and hit-and-run raids against open battles, usually against a superior military force

Haganah a Jewish defence force set up in the 1920s

Holocaust the mass murder of Jews by the Nazis during the Second World War

Intifada a Palestinian uprising against Israeli rule in the Occupied Territories

Islam the religion based on the teachings of the Prophet Mohammad, as laid down in the Koran

Jew one of the Hebrew people descended from the ancient Israelites, a believer in the religion of Judaism

Judaism the religion of the Jews, based on the Old Testament and the Talmud

Knesset parliament of modern Israel

League of Nations an international organization formed in 1919 to settle disputes between states without war; later replaced with the United Nations

militia a loose-knit, non-professional body of fighters

Muslim a follower of the Islamic faith

nationalistic, nationalism the belief that individual communities and cultures should be independent; usually this implies pride in ones country and culture

nomadic continually moving about, with no permanent home

Occupied Territories the areas captured by the Israelis during the 1967 war, the West Bank, Gaza and Jericho

Orthodox conforming to strict and established views and rules in a religion

Ottoman Empire the former Turkish Empire in Europe, Asia and Africa, which lasted from the 13th century until the end of World War One

Palestinian Liberation Organization (PLO) a political and military body set up in 1964 to defend the rights of Palestinian Arabs

Palestinian National Authority the name for the Palestinian government of the West Bank and Gaza territories after self-rule, 1994

Palestinians Arabs expelled from Palestine during the 1948 war

partition division into two or more parts

Passover Jewish festival commemorating the Liberation of the Israelites from Egypt

pogrom the organized massacre of the Jews in Russia

reprisals an action taken in retaliation against an enemy designed to stop them repeating an attack

sanctions banning trade in certain products, e.g. weapons, with a country in order to pressure it into changing policy

secular concerned with social and worldly attitudes rather than religious ones

superpower a country with immense economic and political influence and military (including nuclear) strength; usually refers to the United States and the Soviet Union

United Nations (UN) an international body set up in 1945 as a forum for settling disputes between nations

veto the right or power to reject something in a vote, overruling all other votes

Zionism a form of Jewish nationalism, originally dedicated to the creation of a Jewish state, now supportive of a strong Israel

Zionist a follower of the principles of Zionism

Index